Ashes

by David Rudkin

SAMUEL FRENCH, INC.

25 WEST 45TH STREET   NEW YORK 10036

7623 SUNSET BOULEVARD   HOLLYWOOD 90046

LONDON   *TORONTO*

CAST
(*In Order of Appearance*)

COLIN .... Brian Murray

ANNE .... Roberta Maxwell

MAN .... John Tillinger

WOMAN .... Penelope Allen

TIME: Now

PLACE: England

OPENING NIGHT DECEMBER 7, 1976

MANHATTAN THEATRE CLUB

LYNNE MEADOW—ARTISTIC DIRECTOR
BARRY GROVE—MANAGING DIRECTOR

In Association With

NEW YORK SHAKESPEARE FESTIVAL

JOSEPH PAPP—PRODUCER

present

THE NEW YORK PREMIERE OF

ASHES

by

DAVID RUDKIN

with
(in alphabetical order)

Penelope Allen	**Roberta Maxwell**
Brian Murray	**John Tillinger**

Setting	Lighting
John Lee Beatty	**Dennis Parichy**

Costumes
Jennifer Von Mayrhauser

Sound Design		Sound Design
George Hansen	and	**Charles London**

Dialect Coach	Assistant Director	Production Stage Mgr.
Gordon Jacoby	**Andy Wolk**	**Zane Weiner**

directed by

LYNNE MEADOW

Associate Director	Associate Artistic Director
Thomas Bullard	**Stephen Pascal**

OPENING NIGHT FEBRUARY 8, 1977

ANSPACHER THEATER

JOSEPH PAPP

presents

ASHES

by

David Rudkin

Directed by

Lynne Meadow

with

Penelope Allen   Roberta Maxwell
Brian Murray   John Tillinger

Setting by   *Costumes by*
John Lee Beatty   **Jennifer Von Mayrhauser**

Lighting by   *Sound Design by*
Dennis Parichy   **George Hansen and Charles London**

Associate Producer
Bernard Gersten

A NEW YORK
SHAKESPEARE FESTIVAL PRODUCTION
in association with the
MANHATTAN THEATRE CLUB

*Ashes was originally produced by the Manhattan Theatre Club
and the New York Shakespeare Festival
at the Manhattan Theatre Club.*

CHARACTERS

COLIN: early 30's, Northern Irish, was a writer, now a teacher.

ANNE: late 20's, his wife, West Riding, was an actress, now a teacher.

An averagely presentable couple, neither sexually glamorous nor pathetically unprepossessing. COLIN cared more how he dressed five years ago: a good pair of unflared corduroys he wore for best then, he uses at work today; plain shirt, tie, quilted anorak, hush puppies. ANNE had more style, but now they live far from shops and have less money—a neutral grey smock, fashionable once, now she knocks about in.

OTHER CHARACTERS

DOCTOR
SEMINOLOGIST: ("Guru")
GYNAECOLOGICAL SURGEON
AMBULANCE DRIVER
AREA ADOPTIONS OFFICER
JENNIFER: medical student
RECEPTIONIST: at Guru's
VALERIE: fecund neighbor
NURSE
MRS. JONES: assistant Adoptions Officer

These roles should be taken by one male and one female actor; but in this doubling there is no thematic significance. To cast each separately is possible, but would tell, I think, against the "minimal" method of the play.

STAGING

No set as such is called for. A manoeuverable rostrum Up Right serves as a marriage bed, doctor's couch, ambulance interior, etc., as needed. A simple arrangement of easily drawn white traverse curtains crosses Midstage, to mask, discover, etc., as required. A doctor's desk Down Left, with deep drawers; a microscope. A waste-tin below the desk; a wicker wastebasket near the bed. Three plain upright chairs, one behind desk, others brought by characters as necessary.

The clinical processes shown should be at root authentic, but reduced to a spare theatrical severity. As to the indignities to which COLIN and ANNE submit themselves, they must not make light of them, nor ever clown them; but rather bring us into a wry factual sharing of them. We might here or there be tempted into a tasteless or ignorant laugh: if so, the character must by stillness deliver any necessary rebuke.

The play lasts just over a hundred minutes; and should be given without interval.

Ashes

I

Darkness. From speakers round auditorium, a man's deep rhythmic breathing subsides toward silence. Suddenly from behind screen, thrash and sense of a brief bed tussle—

COLIN. (*Unseen there. Yelp of trivial pain. Voice barely recognizable as Northern Irish: characteristic "ou" and "r" sounds, back "a" sound, hint of Antrim tune.*) Ow no—do you have to do that now?

ANNE. (*Unseen there. Quiet voice, just recognizable as West Riding: trace of back a sound, tune.*) When else do I get? Never still enough.

COLIN. Gouging.

ANNE. Not gouging.

COLIN. Each twinge runs to the knackers like some Turkish torture.

ANNE. (*Mocking.*) Poor knackers . . .

COLIN. Leave over!

ANNE. I've nearly got it . . .

COLIN. (*Threat.*) I'll pull him out—

ANNE. There. A lovely huge one, juicy and black. What was so bad about that?

COLIN. How do you tell in the dark what colour?

ANNE. I've had me eye on that since before we put the lights out.

COLIN. Preying mantis'll never be extinct while you're alive.

ANNE. The human skin must breathe.

COLIN. You've not been aroused by me at all—

ANNE. Don't be fatuous—

COLIN. All my foreplay reefed on your single ex-
pectation of winkling out one clotted pore.

ANNE. I like my man to be healthy.

COLIN. Post-coital triumph more like. Penis jealousy.

ANNE. What? Flatter yourself.

COLIN. (*Pause.*) I never had blackheads till you
started purging them.

ANNE. Not true. (*Pause.*) None of your other bed-
mates bothered, you mean. Whatever sex they were.

COLIN. They: weren't cannibals.

ANNE. (*Pause.*) Getting heavy, love.

COLIN. (*Put out.*) Sorry.

ANNE. (*Pause. Quieter.*) Mop up now.

COLIN. Ay. Load delivered, back to yard, cold half
of bed. (*Sounds of them shifting. Long pause.*)

ANNE. Perhaps we did it this time.

(*SNAP UP STAGELIGHT. White traverse screen
masks all but* ANNE's *half [Right] of bed: on which*
ANNE *lies supine, head toward us, bare legs raised in a
coital posture.* DOCTOR—*fresh-faced, early 30's, slight
hint of the farmer—gently firmly palps her lower belly
to feel that everything is in its proper place.*)

DOCTOR. (*Faintest last trace of rural speech. Frank,
unpatronizing.*) How long have you and your husband
been trying for a conception, Mrs. Harding?

ANNE. Two years.

DOCTOR. Then you *do* have a problem. Forgive me:
you are doing it right?

ANNE. Do we look fools?

DOCTOR. I've had couples trying to conceive through the navel. (*Manipulates, palps.*) No sign of damage or deformity, no displacement . . . Very nice set of organs, Mrs. Harding; compact . . . Your husband is potent, you say; your bloodgroups compatible; your cycle short and regular—

ANNE. (*Bitter.*) Clockwork.

DOCTOR. Which I like. Well. First I think we should take a PC sample—

ANNE. Post-coital.

DOCTOR. (*Surprised she knows.*) Have you been a nurse?

ANNE. No.

DOCTOR. (*Pause. Comes away, peels off a disposable glove into wastebasket.*) Well you can probably work out for yourselves what a post-coital test involves. Round about the tenth or eleventh day of your next cycle— (*CUT LIGHT. In darkness, loud ALARM CLOCK on speakers. Screen fully drawn. Sounds of waking, shifting. CUT ALARM.*)

ANNE. (*Yawning, unseen beyond screen.*) God, what an hour. Why so early?

COLIN. (*Yawning, unseen there.*) Specimen, love.

ANNE. Mm?

COLIN. Specimen. We have to provide a characteristic sample of our mixture. Fresh.

ANNE. (*Miserable, tired.*) Oh fuck—

COLIN. Something like that.

ANNE. I'll have to have a pee. (ANNE *heard stumbling away off beyond screen.*) Put 'fire on, love.

COLIN. (*Grumbles, moving.*) Mouth like a bloody parrot cage . . . (*Slow DIM GLOW as of electric barfire beyond screen: form of* COLIN *before it. LOUD ON SPEAKERS: urine trickling into water; rip, scuff of tissue paper; chain pulled.*) Romantic.

ANNE. (*Dim shape returns there, shuddering.*) Right then. Man. I'm all cold and pissy for you: come and give. (*Lies, head toward screen, raising opened legs in silhouette— Up Stage LIGHT. JENNIFER, student in white coat, moves screen a yard or so Left, discovering DOCTOR standing, bowed, with some unseen medical implement inserted between ANNE's raised legs. A careful snipping sound, then DOCTOR draws implement out, away. JENNIFER helps DOCTOR transfer smear to a slide. DOCTOR peels off disposable glove into wastebasket; JENNIFER brings slide, sets it in microscope. DOCTOR comes, peers into microscope. ANNE, meanwhile, relaxes up into sitting pose on bed's RIGHT side, watches in anxiety.*)

DOCTOR. (*At last.*) Jennifer. (*Very quiet.*)

JENNIFER. Doctor?

DOCTOR. (*Very quiet.*) These sperms are all dead, wouldn't you say?

JENNIFER. (*Looks.*) Oh no, doctor, I think there's one.

DOCTOR. One what?

JENNIFER. One sperm alive.

DOCTOR. Where? (*Looks.*) Where?

JENNIFER. Bottom righthand corner.

DOCTOR. (*Seems at last to find it.*) Oh yes. Oh no. Oh no, Jennifer, that's a hair on the slide. (*Quieter.*) Appointment to see the husband, I think. (*JENNIFER draws screen Right, masking ANNE, part-discovering form of COLIN seated on his side of bed, trousers and briefs down. DOCTOR disposes of smeared slide into waste-tin, draws on another glove, goes up to COLIN. COLIN stands to have his genitals examined. JENNIFER strikes microscope, DOCTOR part-draws screen to pre-*

*serve patient's privacy—*COLIN, *a nether-naked human
form beyond screen's vague translucency.*)

COLIN. The self-consciousness of the situation has
shrunk him rather.

DOCTOR. (*Droll.*) Testicles, not the penis, deliver the
goods. (*To check that testicles are free.*) Cough,
please. (COLIN *coughs.*) Again. (COLIN *coughs.*) No
injury at any time?

COLIN. None.

DOCTOR. No growth, clotting . . .

COLIN. That I know of . . .

DOCTOR. No reason why normal testicles should not
produce good semen. Yet, you know, by the time yours
gets where it matters, your semen is useless. I shall
give you a letter— (*LIGHT CHANGE.* DOCTOR *Off
Above screen.* COLIN *emerges, pulling up briefs, trousers. While as yet keeping us at some distance, he puts
on an act for us:*)

COLIN. (*Imitates a woman receptionist.*) 'Yes, sir,
can I help you?' (*Self.*) I have this letter. It is about
a sperm count. (*Woman.*) 'Oh, this is Family Planning.
You want Fertility. Up the stairs, sir.' (*His trousers
are up now. He looks at us, making us feel a little
easier in his company. Now he goes into another act,
a vocal send-up of a Brummy lab assistant.*) 'Here
y'are then, friend: a room apart. Produce your sample,
bring it back to the lab when yow've done. We send
yow the bill for two smacker, yowr doctor the results
in twenty one days. Venetian blind don't work, I'm
sorry to say, but nobody to overlook yow. Lock on the
door don't work either, I'm sorry to say, but they all
know here what this room is for. (*Confidential.*) Some
blokes has to get their wives to help them wi this at
home, then bring the product in to us by buz. Take

your time.' (COLIN *is staring us out again: his expression never breaks, yet somehow he is charming us into a humorous sharing of his absurd predicament. Yet nothing must rupture his essential privateness. FADE UP SHOUTS, WHISTLINGS, SOUNDS OF BUILDING SITE outside, above;* COLIN *glances up, out toward these once or twice. He takes out of pocket a tiny glass or plastic container—two inches deep at most, neck barely an inch across, with blank label. He looks up from this to us. The building site sounds worry him. And an anatomical problem: how to address an erection to this ludicrous jar? With simple precise gestures he sketches one or two ways that occur to him. Impossible. A third way. Even more absurd. He catches our eye, goes to sit on chair near curtain, plays for time. Has thought: takes out pencil stub, writes on label. Shows us:*) My name. Against confusion. (*Sits, drums fingers. Another idea: puts jar on floor, all but gets down onto all fours above it—* A BUILDER'S VOICE *calling someone above, outside—* COLIN *sharp back on his chair again, jar in hand. CROSSFADE IN CLINIC SOUNDS: trolleys in corridors, someone on intercom calling for a doctor. After a moment,* COLIN *sees he must make a real effort. He brings chair down, drops trousers, turns back on us. Over shoulder, to us:*) What are yous expectin' to see, then? (*Sits. Makes discreetest gesture of fondling; then suddenly a little tsk-tsk sound as though geeing up a diminutive horse between his thighs there. Soon, gentle:*) There's a fella. There's a fella. (*Sound of door opened, shriek of young girl—* COLIN *sharply rises, hands covering himself. Clattering heels flee, a stifled giggle; giggles shared afar. Over shoulder, to us:*) Was ever fella so abused? (*CROSSFADE IN*

BUILDING SITE SOUNDS, jolly whistling, etc. An idea: To penis.) We'll go an take a look at the builder boys. There's maybe a nice arse'll turn ye on. (*Part-hauling trousers up, makes off above screen—Suddenly comes hurrying back for jar. Off AGAIN. CUT SOUNDS. LIGHT CHANGE. From where* COLIN *went now,* DOCTOR *comes, labelled jar in hand, now containing a milky dreg. Goes to sit behind desk:*)

DOCTOR. Colin Harding, his seed. There's life in this, the clinic tells me: though not so much as I should like. (COLIN, *dressed again, comes round screen Right, brings chair to sit before desk.*) You could conceive with this semen, Mr. Harding; but it would be a miracle.

COLIN. (*No aggression; acceptance merely.*) You mean my seed is sterile?

DOCTOR. No. A hundred or so million sperms per millilitre a man ejaculates when making love: only one of these need reach the ovum, to conceive. But all X hundred million need to be very lively, for there to be that chance.

COLIN. Mine are not—lively.

DOCTOR. Too few of them are. They litter this fluid like so many stunned tadpoles, I'm afraid.

COLIN. (*Pause.*) Can anything be done. (*NB. almost no question tone.*)

DOCTOR. You can help. Use a shower from now, not a bath. Scrap your tight briefs for boxer shorts. It takes six weeks to make a sperm, and requires a temperature in the scrotum two degrees lower than that of the body. Which is why in hot weather, you will have noticed, your ballocks dangle. Circulation. So, every morning and every evening for the next six weeks, bathe your testicles in the coldest water, sev-

eral minutes at a time. At the end of January, go back
for another sperm count. Central heating, you know,
probably reduces male fertility more than any other
factor in the West. I think, also, you should eat less:
hunger helps fecundity. (COLIN *turns to us, an I-ask-
you gesture; LIGHT CHANGE.*)

COLIN. Hands up who's tried bathing his balls.
Dangle them in a bowl, do I hear ye say? Some
anatomy: you try that. (DOCTOR *meanwhile disposes
of semen jar into waste-tin; goes Off.*) A washcloth,
then? Not very effective. Stand akimbo in the bath, a
cold shower aimed upwards? (*Mimes this. Mimes
getting soaked.*) One foot outside the bath, then, the
other across? (*Mimes this, chair as bath.*) Marginally
improved for access: if you don't mind cleaning the
floor down twice a day. I doubt even a bidet's not
much help, in my precise predicament. But, for those
of you, for those of you who may at some time need
it, a solution does emerge. Sit back on the bog pan,
your legs priapically wide; grip the showerhead in one
hand, in the other exposing the scrotum to its full,
freezing blast. December. Friends in the house over
Christmas— (*Birmingham speech.*) 'Mom, what's that
funny splashing in the bathroom?' The things a silly
sod'll do for fatherhood. Or is it fatherhood. Or is it
fatherhood? Might it not rather be, for the myth of
'manliness'? (*Exits Down Stage Left.* ANNE *seen,
comes down with letters.*)

ANNE. Enter wife, reading aloud for audience's
benefit several convenient letters. Marj is expecting.
Valerie is expecting. Cynthia's in pod again. None of
them planned for. Wendy miscounts on the pill;
Hilary's Albert comes home from a police course randy
as hell, no time for precautions, wham bam thank you

ma'am, hey ho another bottle shot from the shelf. Click from a man's pants, some women. (*Last letter.*) From the doctor. Sperm motility now normal, quote: if you go overdue, inform me. After three or four months I do. First time in my bleeding life, overdue. I say, no, it's a freak. Or hysterical. Twenty-nine days, for me unheard of. Thirty. He's telling himself, stop thinking about it, stop hoping: watched pot and that. We've clicked or we haven't. Thirty-one days. If we can hang on till only Monday, hang out the flags, I'm qualifying for a Urine Test! Thirty-two days. Every time I'm out of the room now, I can hear his ears pricked for the sound of the door of the cupboard where I keep my pads. Thirty-third day. No gutrot. No pain in the back, no heaviness in the breasts. Just the blood. (*Pause. Sits.* COLIN *comes quietly.*)

COLIN. Bad one? (*He doesn't need telling. He reaches, touches her: but there is nothing in the touch; in the tenderness is something hard, hurt.* ANNE *turns head from him, moves her Colinward hand across herself from him: remains so, frozen, unpresent. Enter* GURU: *greying short hair, fine-rimmed spectacles, Edinburgh accent of professional class.*)

GURU. (*To us.*) I am an expensive seminologist. My two new patients dub me the Guru because they get the impression I think I am omniscient. Indeed, I do occasionally speak as though I personally had invented the first idea of everything, including coitus itself. (*Sits behind desk.* GURU's *lady* RECEPTIONIST, *impeccably manicured, the type to make a man feel he reeks of sweat, comes for* COLIN.)

RECEPTIONIST. Mr. Harding?

COLIN. (*Follows her.*) Colin Harding, yes, I have an appointment—Doctor Mc—

RECEPTIONIST. I'm sure your accent will make Doctor McAnespie feel quite at home. What part of Scotland are you from?

COLIN. Belfast.

RECEPTIONIST. (*Pause.*) Not a very happy place, these days. (COLIN *can say nothing to that.* RECEPTIONIST *leaves him seated opposite* GURU; *moves screen along Right, masking* ANNE; *continues Off.* GURU *now has file of letters on desk before him.*)

COLIN. Doctor, I am not a superstitious man. Forgive me if this question sounds benighted. My very first erotic urges—the earliest I remember—were to bite lumps out of classmates' buttocks in the showers: especially the hairier ones, as I myself was never very hairily endowed. I'm still tormented with a ravening homosexual self.

GURU. (*Gentle.*) Oh, there is no such thing as a 'homosexual self.' Sexuality runs deeper than culture, how can it discriminate; why should it, as culture does? You have a sexual self. That is your central essential energy, deeper, truer than any cultural self: homo- and hetero- are straws on the surface. A single-sex school you were at?

COLIN. Oh, a day one, but very ancient: the usual seedbed of gentle Christian fascism. The cult of the Chap, the heroic unattainable ideal: from which regime an inadequate like me is expected at nineteen, miraculously, to blossom straight. Ten years of my adult emotional life that schooling cost me, ten maimed years: I know where I would put a bomb if a Fenian ever gave me one. No child of mine must ever go to such a place. I fought hard—not to convert my sexuality from one orientation to another, but to broaden it to include the opposite sex as well. I refused to be the stunted end of a tree. A hard fight; I have won. My sexual world is very discordant now, but for all the vain yearning my several lusts put me in, I am glad in their diversity and would not be without one of them. Out from this all, my wife is the best thing has happened to me. Now we want children. For years we have had no luck, and it is inexplicable— you have the history of it there. So I ask this. It will sound naive, but this is now something of a mortal strait for me, and when our back is to the wall we think irrational things: can there be, can there be at all any causality, any connection, between the homo-erotics I still also so strongly feel, and the dying of my seed?

GURU. If you believe in a crabbed heterosexual father-God, you could call your plight a Judgment. If you believe what you are paying me seven old guineas for, then I, as a man of reason and acquainted with chemistry, say, No cause, no cause. Just stretch the skin tighter over your testicles when you bathe them; and two minutes only, twice in the day. Continue the cold water, until you have conceived.

COLIN. But could worry, or stress of any kind— Or if my work were not going well, or I were at some professional crisis— (GURU *checks through letter before him, to see what* COLIN's *profession is.*) Could anything emotional or psychological—

GURU. (*A slight impatience.*) Mr. Harding: you do perform the sexual act?

COLIN. Yes.

GURU. And you ejaculate?

COLIN. Yes.

GURU. Well. Man's piddling little psyche might hinder performance, but not affect one whit the chemical quality of what he secretes. The trouble in your case most possibly lies with neither wife nor you, but in the combination of your genetic chemistries. (*Stands.*) You are familiar with the routine for the post-coital test?

COLIN. We have done several. (*Stands.*)

GURU. (*Looks at letter.*) Here also your diligence has been excessive: there is no need for the alarm clock, intercourse the night before is quite sufficient. (RECEPTIONIST *re-enters Up Right;* GURU *brings* COLIN *Up Left;* RECEPTIONIST *draws screen Right, discovering* ANNE, *on bed.*) Semen is petrol, the engine is the womb: the one must merely be brought, effective, to the other. I recommend you now, during the fertile period of Mrs. Harding's month, to adopt for intercourse what I call a posture of performing dogs— (RECEPTIONIST *charmingly invites:* ANNE *poses as* GURU *describes:*) Your wife on her knees, head down, her buttocks spread—

ANNE. (*To us.*) Dignity. (RECEPTIONIST *bows* ANNE's *head;* GURU *brings* COLIN *behind her*—)

GURU. You entering from behind. Which may, in your case, revive certain unorthodox memories. Nevertheless— (*Motions* COLIN *to kneel closer behind* ANNE, *almost to mount her.* RECEPTIONIST, *meanwhile, brings a larger-than-life anatomy class phallus, vertically sectioned, one side all vein and stem, the other all tubes, a similar corset-model of female genitalia.*) You will see how, in this posture, the female tackle flops, affording the penis— (RECEPTIONIST *inserts phallus: a clicking of parts*—) the most efficient angle of insemination. Compared with which, the conventional Anglo-American attitude— (RECEPTIONIST *withdraws phallus,* GURU *rights corset:* RECEPTIONIST *inserts again, click, click, click*—) from the spermatozoön's point of view, is all uphill. (COLIN, ANNE *remain postured—clinical objects.*) It's all yours.

COLIN. You'll send us the bill?

RECEPTIONIST. Of course. (RECEPTIONIST, GURU *go*— COLIN *starts in*—GURU *re-emerges:*)

GURU. Mr. Harding, one other thing. We may of course be wrong in assuming your sperm count adequate— (COLIN, *interrupted*—) I'm not altogether satisfied with the procedure at that clinic— (RECEPTIONIST *follows, bringing to* COLIN *a ludicrously thin little tube*—) Would you therefore, as early as you feel able, observing the necessary three days' continence beforehand, be good enough to furnish a sample at your home, returning it well sealed to me by post, first class? I can then do a count myself before I come to the PC test to see what, if anything, ill-befalls your semen in your wife. (*Goes;* RECEPTIONIST *follows.* COLIN *stands away with tube addressing us, coming down:*)

COLIN. Up again, down again: Jack found fecund, now his fecundity in question, now branded barren. (*Developing a tone of mocking self-laceration.*) So, if Jack's lust does after all lack living spore, this seems to Jack wondrous like Nature does not select him for the Club of Man—the sort, I mean, Nature prefers not to continue his kind. I learned to live with that emotion a long time since. Yet: might not Nature's very discardment of Jack rank Jack a little higher than the genital beast in Man? *More* man than Reproductive Man? Paradox. Think. Jack's seed, qua sterile, is fit for transcendental sport alone; made not for breeding, but delight alone; to be shot singing out, anarchic, athletic, milk in itself, free up vagina and glad up lad-arse, knob cleaving cunt for joy alone, splitting sphincter and reaming rectum for joy alone, his bags drained through holes in walls by unseen men's mouths: the naked jissom, dis-Communion-ized, for play alone. (*More quiet.*) Perhaps there is some sort of evolution here: man's sex emancipated from the shackle and the mire of Propagation; a sexuality dis-familied, detribalized, *fraternal*: in this sterility, the seed of that? (COLIN *goes up to bed, kneels behind* ANNE *upon it; wearily removes anorak as they posture themselves.*)

ANNE. He functions to order every time. Only once, for the Guru's PC, he couldn't stay hard, it wouldn't penetrate— Surprised? You try it to order on two or three fixed nights in the cycle: knowing 'Tonight or never; the love-blend must be there for the doctor to-morrow; or for hope of conception this month. Or for doctor, anyway.' In this posture. He probably has to pretend I'm some sailor from his misspent youth.

COLIN. (*Makes to mount her.*) The acts don't re-semble, lovey. Though it is possible to fantasize: which, frankly, at times has helped me. (*Suddenly sighs, falls away, lies wretched.*)

ANNE. Anyway, this one time, for the Guru's PC, he just couldn't stay hard enough to enter. Every effort of mine just made him floppier. (*She slowly, meanwhile, rests back upon her hunkers, more and more relaxing him, generating simply by tenderness and voice a deeply erotic mood.*) But in the night, in his sleep, he was starting me. I woke up so turned on. After a while I went down on him—it was the first time I had ever been moved to do that. He'd come up very heavy and strong: the knob felt so burgeoning and gorgeous. So, half-asleep, we managed it after all. So we've never in all these years—for doctor or calendar—never once failed to deliver. On occasions like the one I describe; he can be quite a satyr. Appearances deceive.

COLIN. It's better at such times, love, the better you help me.

ANNE. (*Not breaking mood till very end.*) I thought after that one, I thought if the quality of the act itself has anything to do with it and we haven't clicked this time, then there's no fucking justice in the thing. (*Bitterly lies away;* GURU *comes, brisk, quiet; draws screen across* COLIN; *comes to* ANNE; *gently, firmly postures her lying on left side, right leg crooked up.* ANNE *continues to us:*) This man is a *specialist.* He examines in the Sims position. Not like your National Health. (*Lies so for examination.* GURU *makes minimal sufficient gestures of examination: touch palp pressure, etc.*)

GURU. Your husband's sperms are now of normal vitality, Mrs. Harding. Yet by the time they percolate here— (*Pats her lower belly.*) a great proportion of them are dead. You would seem to be killing your husband's semen, Mrs. Harding: why is that? (*There has been no cruelty in his tone, merely a philosophical mildly-rebuking gentleness.* ANNE *can say nothing.*) The medical profession has no answer in such a case. It may be, that some form of chemical rejection is taking place—

ANNE. (*Clutching at joyous straw.*) Something to do with antigens?

GURU. (*Looks at her stilly, says nothing. Then:*) This is a terra incognita of medical science. There is a broader possibility. In intercourse, the vagina produces a self-protecting acid. Sperms do not like this acid. The acid, therefore, not only helps prevent infection, it also acts as a goad to the sperms to hasten them on their way. Perhaps your vagina is producing too much acid, or too strong. Relax . . . (*Comes away to sit behind desk. Quiet, to self:*) So many good spermatozoa dead.

ANNE. (*Relaxes up, semi-sitting.*) Massacre of the Innocents.

GURU. Unjust, yes. Your doing, but not your fault.

ANNE. If I shove my fanny full of bicarb before we sex, would that do any good? (*Comes to desk.*)

GURU. (*Does not like being anticipated.*) I was coming to the alkaline douche. (*Brings from a drawer in desk, a package.*) This is a little something of my own invention. Bicarbonate of soda is, yes, safe, and domestically available. But do remember you thereby expose your vagina to infection. So be moderate (*Gives package.*)

ANNE. (*Sitting.*) Perhaps we should just accept our infertility as our part played in easing an overpopulated world.

GURU. And be content to leave the breeding to village yobs, clapped-out royalty and Papish slums? While the psychopaths that misgovern our globe make waste and slag of its sufficiency?

ANNE. I don't like to think of people in terms of absolute worth.

GURU. Then start to think so. You know your Malthus as well as I do: the one inheritance Man is short in is Reason. Even if you and your husband look like the back end of buses, you've more than an average share of Reason to bequeath. That is your duty to the world. If Man is to survive, he must evolve up out of his mythic mire; and soon. So tell your husband to keep up the cold water treatment and the diet; and you combine the posture and the alkali. We'll get you a bun in the oven for Christmas Eve. (*Briskly goes*

Off Up Right, swinging screen Right, discovering all bed—)

COLIN. (*Discovered on bed.*) Another seven old guineas, that sets us back. (ANNE *undoes package: a comically flopping douche device.*)

ANNE. And this, another two. (*Squeezes nozzle, makes gurgling sounds with mouth.* COLIN *comes to her. They lark with douche; suddenly, as though afraid of losing their sexuality forever, are in desperate, almost childish play.*) I wish we could get back to sex for kicks.

COLIN. (GURU *voice.*) 'You are not one of those fortunates, Mrs. Harding, that can conceive with "kicks": accept that. You might yet need recourse to my inseminator, a Heath Robinson device I've invented for ferrying live sperms through no-go areas.' (*Mood suddenly broken:* ANNE *remembers what douche is for.* COLIN: *new note of hardness ill-suppressed.*) Give fanny her gargle, then. (ANNE *goes off with douche.*) While I lie, lashing up salacious thoughts of the utmost crudity to sustain my erection, my heart knocks like a stone with the false effort. . . . Till you come from the bathroom, cold as ice— (ANNE *returns, adopts a posture on bed—*)

ANNE. To squat before my lord, my arse on high like Table Mountain.

COLIN. (*Raises self on knees behind her.*) And I must start upon you straightaway. . . . (*Reaches hands beneath her oxters.*) And get my pint pulled up you straightaway. . . . (*CUT LIGHT OFF. In darkness, loud on speakers: SOUNDS of a fruit-machine, being played, rhythmic, dry, mechanical, luckless. UP LIGHT.*)

ANNE. Being not sure how long or short the antacid effect of the bicarb will last—

COLIN. To say nothing of the fact this bloody posture is giving me piles.

ANNE. Why can't we make like the amoeba?

COLIN. Split in two?

ANNE. Or freeze in a cyst, then explode in little hundreds.

COLIN. Defeat the object, wouldn't it?

ANNE. What is the object? (*They remain coupled, motionless, faces toward us.*)

COLIN. To think we were a year on the pill before we married.

ANNE. (*To us.*) Repeat on the thirteenth and fifteenth nights of the cycle. Two cycles. Five.

COLIN. (*Slowly withdrawing.*) Remembering always to come away carefully, not spilling any. (*Lies away from her, speaking over pillow to us.*) Sacrament, my arse. Four stages of a childless marriage. 'Children?' (*Mild.*) 'Not yet.' 'Children?' (*Slightly rebuking.*) 'Give us time.' 'Children?' (*Gentle, sad.*) 'No.' 'Children?' (*Defiant, i.e. Should there be?*) 'No.'

ANNE. (*Relaxes up into Little Mermaid pose, drawing blanket round self, facing Right.*) 'Try changing the wallpaper,' they say. Aunts, mother-in-law, sisters. 'It's nothing to do with the *function*,' I tell them: 'that part of it's all right.' (*Now appears behind her a Young Married, VALERIE, nursing baby and obscenely pregnant, a mixture of the affected-vulgar and intellectual pretension:*)

VALERIE. Try buying some different coloured nighties, dear.

ANNE. I've told you, Valerie: that part's in order!

VALERIE. Get him away, a romantic holiday, a second honeymoon—or would it be the third or fourth, dear, including those you had with him before you were married?

ANNE. It's nothing—

VALERIE. George had his troubles, too. A warm climate's the thing—

ANNE. It's chemistry, Valerie. Not the sex, the chemistry.

VALERIE. Perhaps he should take up football. On second thoughts, perhaps not, knowing his past. (*Disappears.*)

ANNE. (*Almost tearful.*) It's nothing to do with that! It's chemistry! (*Settles in blanket again.*) Women. Young Marrieds. Shriek to each other across their prams. Joggle their dummystuffed spoils of the sex war up and down. Trundle along their suburban bellies bloated with the booty of the bed. 'How far are you on then, Doreen? Five months? Oh, I'm six.' Cows. The only function they're up to, so they crack it high: cows, cows. They look at me. '*You* haven't pillaged your breadwinner's basket in the dark when he thinks he's polishing the top sheet with his arse; *you* haven't ignited a brat; *you're* no woman, *you're* inadequate.' I get to hate my parasitic sex. (*Now comes down past them to desk, a* GYNAECOLOGICAL SURGEON: *smooth, groomed, impeccably dressed in conservative fashion. He has a medical file, quite full by now.* COLIN, ANNE *assemble themselves.*)

SURGEON. But in all these years of consultation, no one has thought to confirm if you are in fact ovulating, Mrs. Harding. (*To us.*) Gynaecological surgeon, their last resort. (*Sits behind desk.* COLIN, ANNE *come down, sit: she opposite* SURGEON, COLIN *at desk-end, between them.*) No point in pumping your poor husband dry, if there is no egg for him to fertilize. (*Takes slim packet from drawer.*) So, with your next cycle, you must begin a regular taking of your morning temperature on waking, entering it each day with a cross on this chart. (*Brings out from drawer a quarto buff envelope, from which he takes blank temperature-charts, stage-large.* COLIN, ANNE *furtively glance at each other, reduced.*) If, round about your tenth day or so, the graph you are making suddenly dips, say five or six points of a degree, and the next day rises again by as much and a little more, you can normally assume ovulation has occurred. Whereupon, I recommend you two initiate an orgy. After six months, if you have indeed not conceived before then, make an appointment to bring me the charts, so that I can see what ovulation-pattern, if any, is suggested by them. It is helpful also if you ring the graph-points on dates when intercourse has taken place. (*Looks at top letter in file.*) Bicarbonate of soda. Yes. Used in moderation, possibly quite helpful; though useless of course without ovulation, I think you understand that. Antacid effectiveness in the vagina, lasts quite some hours. You could douche yourself at leisure during the evening; earlier, even. (*Glances at letter again:*) Posture. Circus dogs, you call it. (*Shakes head.*) Unless you enjoy it that way. It makes mechanical sense, but has not, in my experience, significantly increased the chances of conception in a case like yours. One thing your letter does not make clear: your sperm counts, were they of motility only? Not of volume?

COLIN. Not of volume. That I know of.

SURGEON. I don't mean the quantity of the load, I mean its density in sperms. Your sperms can be the most motile under heaven, but if they are few, say a mere fifty million per millilitre, then all the cold water in the world will not make you fertile.

COLIN. I know the drill.

SURGEON. (*Bringing up from drawer a long printed envelope that slightly bulges.*) Good. The more sperms you put into circulation at any one time, the better your chances, I think you see that. The contents are self-explanatory: two forms, a sealable container. By post to the Path Lab, or drop it by: for this purpose a time-lag will not matter; even if all the sperms die in the post, it is merely a question of our counting the corpses. (COLIN *takes envelope,* ANNE *charts.*) If that, and these, are in order, I see no reason why the two of you should not be expectant by midsummer.

COLIN. You will send the bill.

SURGEON. Yes. And the charts and the thermometer together will come to an extra eighty pence. (*Stands, quiet, to go.*) Don't be despondent. (*Goes. In LIGHT CHANGE,* ANNE *goes, sits on bedfoot with charts. Traces their reading with thermometer.* COLIN *remains in half-light, seated at desk-end.*)

ANNE. Sixteenth of February, sixth day of the cycle: ninety-seven point nine, sexed. (*With thermometer, seems to trace her entries on chart.*) Seventeenth of February, ninety-seven point seven. Eighteenth of February, blank: faulty thermometer. Ninth day of cycle, new thermometer, temperature ninety-eight. Ninety-seven point nine, sexed. Point six, point six. Blank—dropped thermometer. Ninety-eight . . . Sixteenth day of cycle, up: ninety-nine point three. Point two, sexed; sore throat and cold; point four . . . Four, three, three . . . Twenty-eighth day of cycle, point eight again. Period. (COLIN *looks across at* ANNE's *bowed head, hard in spite of himself. She scans charts as though for sign of life; finds none. To us:*) They assure us it's neither's *fault.* Yet now it seems because of his deficiency, now because of mine. That gets at you. The combination of our chemistries, they say. Yet now it seems his fault, now it seems mine. (*Sits with charts, demoralized.* COLIN, *at desk-end, mimes speech into phone.*)

COLIN. I only want to find out if you have the *result* yet. But it has been rather a long time—it was not a motility test, madam, it was a density test. Hell—the analysis must surely have been done by now. . . . I am not trying, madam, to tell pathology their job; I merely wish you would credit other professions than yours with some scintilla of intelligence . . . All I want to know— (*Pause.*) But I am not asking for the result, I am merely trying to establish whether there yet is one, and how soon my doctor may expect to receive it . . . (*Pause.*) I *am* aware your wheels rotate at an inflexible speed— God, this is England all over: —Can you merely estimate roughly, how long, from donation of sample, a man must wait for the alimentary process of your hospital to excrete a result?— For the lord's sake, woman, it *is my sperm.* . . . (*Re-enter simply, quiet,* SURGEON *to desk: he has a letter.*)

SURGEON. Excellent. Perfectly satisfactory. Average, not more; but normally fertile. What more could you reasonably demand? (COLIN, ANNE *meanwhile sit before him again.* SURGEON *turns to* ANNE *and her charts:*)

SURGEON. Now, here what have we? What are these? (ANNE *shoves charts before him.* SURGEON *cannot join them up; he seems to find them scruffy. Suddenly,* ANNE *is as vulnerable as a pathetic slum child before an irascible teacher.*) How do these connect? (ANNE *tries to organize them; they become a muddle.*) February . . . Where is March? (ANNE, SURGEON *search in vain.* COLIN, ANNE *clumsily change places.*) This blot: what happened here?

ANNE. Thermometer broke.

SURGEON. April . . . Where is March? (COLIN *watches this with tense amazement,* SURGEON *points to funny marks on chart:*) What are these diamonds?

ANNE. (*Peers.*) Pencil broke. It broke when I was doing a circle. For when we'd sexed. So I turned the circle into a diamond. Because of the scratch. So I turned them all into diamonds. (SURGEON *holds up chart: it is larger than life-size, with diamond marks clustered in fours and fives mid-cycle, blanks elsewhere. Then:*)

SURGEON. Where is March? (*It is found.* SURGEON *arranges charts along ros-top:*) Now we have a chronology. (*Waves to* ANNE *to sit near him where she can follow.*) Yes . . . (*Ponders.*) A slightly erratic ovulation pattern; but it is there. Look, March, then July; this month . . . You're still on the water?

COLIN. (*Suddenly stammering.*) Y-yes. Two minutes every—

SURGEON. (*To her.*) And the antacid douche?

COLIN. Just as you t- As you t-old us, you— (*Irrational long pause.*)

SURGEON. Well . . . (*Pause.*) Well then, why aren't we conceiving? All that, in conjunction with these . . . (*I.e. charts.*)

COLIN. (*Sudden nervous fatuity.*) It's all rather like planning a moonshot.

SURGEON. (*Ignores him.*) With all this, the odds now are, you should hit the jackpot before the end of the year. I frankly see nothing else I nor anyone can do, except leave it to nature's blind will, with your rational assistance. (*Collects charts, clips them in file.*) You have approached the problem with realism and courage: I am sure your pertinacity will be rewarded. (*LIGHT DIM,* SURGEON *quietly going.*)

COLIN. (*Turning "through" us.*) Ay. In time to pick up our pensions on the way. (*Darkness. Soon, shapes of* COLIN *asleep,* ANNE *on bed appear in silhouette on screen.* ANNE *has thermometer in mouth, then reads it. Soon she begins to cluck like a hen.* COLIN *wakes, stirs:*)

COLIN. What's up wi *you?*

ANNE. I've laid an egg. I've laid an egg!

COLIN. Hang out the flags.

ANNE. (*Rising over him.*) An innocent ovum: has descended the Fallopian. Come and get it.

COLIN. I see. I'm in for a week of phallic martyrdom then am I? (*Darkness. On* SPEAKERS, *fruit-machine* SOUNDS. *Suddenly a triumphant cataclysm of money.* CUT. *Voices of* DOCTOR *Up Right.* JENNIFER, *Off Down Left, call across dark stage to each other:*)

DOCTOR. Jennifer?

JENNIFER. Doctor?

DOCTOR. Mrs. Harding's urine sample: did you test it?

JENNIFER. Yes.

DOCTOR. What shall I tell her?

JENNIFER. Tell her positive. (*ORGAN, ORCHES-TRA, CHOIR titanically BURST OUT: first half-dozen bars MAHLER VIII, "Veni, veni Creator Spiritus." UP PENCIL SPOT on desk now draped altar-like with white cloth, central on it a tall specimen jar, chalice-like, filled with straw-coloured liquid. TIGHTEN SPOT on jar till it glows like Holy Grail. Brutally in mid-paean, CUT MUSIC, LIGHT. Silence, darkness. Follow as soon as practically possible with:*)

*Rapid bare piano-octaves, reiterated clattering grim
(Schubert: Der ErlKönig). In darkness strike jar,
cloth, desk; draw screen fully across, a white en-
closing arc. Fade Schubert (before voice enters),
up stonechat-, finch-song—discreetly soft-centred
sound, intentionally 'lyrical.' Up warm sunlight.
ANNE lies in smock on naked ground (NB no
blanket), COLIN, in trousers, open shirt, Up of her,
lazily stroking her belly. The tenderness is between the three of them: man, woman, and unborn child. He tries to remember words of a poem
(in fact Traherne's Salutation), can manage only
a halting garble:*

COLIN. (*To self.*) What shall this be? That out of
nothing comes . . . Who, dust a thousand years . . .
did in a chaos lie . . . (*Puts ear to her belly. His
caress and wonder broaden, including* ANNE *herself.
After a moment, softly whistles a strain of Brigg Fair.
Suddenly, to us:*) So bloody English, this. All we
need's a bit of Delius offstage.

ANNE. (COLIN'S *stroking begins to show sexual in-
tent.*) Not here, love—

COLIN. Why?

ANNE. People—

COLIN. Who? Who's to see? No one comes up *this*
hill any more—

ANNE. (*Mock Northern.*) Man wi telescope.

COLIN. Let him. (*Careful of* ANNE'S *precious burden,
becomes more sexually purposeful.*)

33

ANNE. (*Shifts in sudden discomfort.*) Trouble with being Lawrentian. Ants and—spines . . . Sorry, love, I'll have to pee first. This weight.

COLIN. A heavy bladder is a stimulus to me.

ANNE. Difference between us. (*Moving from him.*)

COLIN. (*Draws her firmly down.*) I'm damn glad we're *not* the amoeba. (*They deepkiss. After a long moment* ANNE *goes up, waddling slightly, behind screen.* COLIN *lies languorous; with discreet private gesture, fingers luxuriously stretched and hooking, suggest the deep still glory of his resurrected shaft, reburgeoned testicles. Searches memory for poem again.*) Who shall . . . who shall he or she be . . .? that out of nothing comes . . . A nothing: that all a sudden—is . . . Where there was empty darkness, a sudden eye, seeing . . . Sudden in emptiness, new-minted limbs. Out of the dark silence, a forming tongue . . . Child— (*Ulsterish.*) Jamie . . . or (*Ulsterish:*) Annie . . . (*Silence.* ANNE *emerging, afraid to move. Something wrong.* COLIN *turns sharply to her.*)

ANNE. (*Quiet, hard.*) No sex. Get me home. I'm passing these. (*Thrusts into his, our sight, a white tissue in her cupped hands. In it, black clots of blood. A moment. Shock goes off in* COLIN *like a deep mine— no other reaction shown. CUT LIGHT. In darkness, silence, strike screen altogether;* COLIN *Off. Up gloomy indoor LIGHT. Stage bare but for bed Up Right, its foot toward us now. Right of bed, her back ever toward us,* ANNE *donning white nightdress, being helped into bed by* DOCTOR *(of opening scenes) now in coat. To Left of bed, indistinct, an upright chair on which a jacket, tie, dressing gown, etc.*)

DOCTOR. (*Quiet.*) How far are you on now, Mrs. Harding?

ANNE. Three months.

DOCTOR. Well; this is what we call a Pregnancy at Risk.

ANNE. (*Into bed.*) What must we do?

DOCTOR. Stay in bed until forty-eight hours after the bleeding stops.

ANNE. It will stop?

DOCTOR. It'll have to stop some time. You haven't an inexhaustible supply. (*Quietly goes Off Right. LIGHT CHANGE, COLIN coming slowly down with waste-basket full with dark-stained bloody tissues.*)

COLIN. (*To us.*) And such blood. The clots of it, claret-colour, solid-soft. The child is lost. I don't mean I foresee that—we'll do everything mortal possible to prevent that. I mean, it is now that in the heart the loss takes place. (*He is going to say something more. Decides not to. Goes up slowly toward bed with basket. LIGHT CHANGE, DOCTOR comes quietly Right in hat, with case. ANNE lies under bedclothes, head on high pillow, facing us. DOCTOR rests bag on bed.*)

DOCTOR. So what happened this time, Mrs. Harding?

ANNE. I lay as you said. The blood stopped. It dried. It came up brown and fibry. I saved you— (*She makes as to bring out a tissue with it from under pillow— DOCTOR gestures no need.*) Thank God we got the spuds in before this happened.

DOCTOR. Spuds in already?

ANNE. He uses the Ulster calendar. In Patrick's day, out Billy's day. Well then I got up. I helped put in the tomato plants—well *that's* not strenuous.

COLIN. (*Returning, hovers with basket.*) I did the digging. I thought this year to water the soil very heavily at the start. Drive the roots down . . . (*Real-*

izes he is chattering. Puts basket by bed, goes Off Right.)

ANNE. In the night I felt wet. Blood again: red, bright; fresh. Bed rest. Dry again; forty-eight clear hours, then up again. *No* exertion this time. We're going out: I clean myself up. Blood again. Bed again. Dry again, up again, blood again; bed again. Doctor, that drug—there's a drug—

DOCTOR. Our pharmacy shelves are full of that, we never prescribe it now. It seals you up. If you *insist* . . . But if there's a good reason for a foetus to miscarry then miscarry we must let it. I know you have very much wanted this child, but you at least know now how you can conceive.

ANNE. I'm not that young.

DOCTOR. Nonsense.

ANNE. If it takes that long again I'll be over thirty. What you call it? An 'elderly primate.' Superannuated ape.

DOCTOR. You won't find a good apple dropped from a tree. If that sounds like corny rural wisdom, it is nevertheless so. Things happen in their time.

ANNE. Doctor, what chance?

DOCTOR. Fifty fifty.

ANNE. As bad as that?

DOCTOR. Try to keep calm. Stay in bed now. (*Closes bag, goes.* COLIN, *paler-faced, wheels in a Variett-style table—height adjustable: on it, cereals in dish, a boiled egg, bread, coffeepot, marmalade.*)

COLIN. (*Slightly hard.*) How's the blood?

ANNE. (*Takes clean tissue from under pillow; explores with it beneath blankets; withdraws it.*) Started again. (*Shows him reddened tissues, almost flinching.*)

COLIN. (*Face hard, still. Wheels table so that it lies across her like a tray.*) I'm not sure about the egg.

ANNE. What do you mean, 'not sure about the egg?'

COLIN. Well it's the second one. The first floated. Even this one tried to turn its wide end up.

ANNE. (*Sees it is missing.*) Salt.

COLIN. Sorry. (*Goes.*)

ANNE. (*Shouts after.*) I don't like the eggs from Clay Hall Farm, they taste of fish. God knows what they feed their poultry on. (*Sprays sugar on cereal. COLIN comes with salt.*) Darling, I'm sorry, you've forgotten the spoon.

COLIN. Sorry. (*Goes.*)

ANNE. (*Shouts.*) Why don't you get the eggs from Clink Farm? (*Crunches teeth into cereal.*)

COLIN. (*Returns with teaspoon.*) Because Clink is out of my way. (*Snatches tie from chair, half-threads it on.*)

ANNE. Oh not that spoon, dear, for eggs; they stain. The Apostle spoons.

COLIN. Sorry, I didn't think. (*Goes.*)

ANNE. (*Shouts.*) Well how many times have you eaten an egg and not noticed what spoon you're using?

COLIN. (*Returns.*) Judas, that do you? I'll go and have my own now— (*Tray tilts over, spilling; ANNE screaming, saves coffeepot, egg, holds these transfixed.*) That's all I need.

ANNE. Who didn't tighten the sodding screw? (*COLIN rights tray, tightens screw; restores what order he can. Bread-and-butter loathsomely dirtied on floor.*) You're treading the cornflakes in—

COLIN. Well either you— (*I.e., want me to tighten the table.*)

ANNE. Well don't. Oh hell, there's milk on the blankets—

COLIN. Well I'm sorry— Use a tissue— A tissue—! (*Etc.*)

ANNE. It'll come through to the sheets, love. I can't lie in wet sheets: sponge it off, quickly— A sponge, love; quickly—! (*Etc.* COLIN *exits,* ANNE *dabs with tissues.* COLIN *returns with sponge. They dab.*)

COLIN. You'll need more milk now. (*Goes.*)

ANNE. I'll eat the cornflakes dry, I'll drink the coffee black!

COLIN. (*Off.*) Don't be silly. (*Cry of despair.*) Oh no! No!

ANNE. (*Shouts.*) What is it?

COLIN. (*Off, furious.*) Out. Out. Out! *Out!* (*Pause.*)

ANNE. What's happened?

COLIN. (*Comes with milk bottle.*) Excuse jug. Two pieces of news. First the good. The cat has puked. (*Goes Off.*)

ANNE. Feed her properly, she won't.

COLIN. (*Off.*) She's perfectly fittingly fed.

ANNE. You give her too much hard tack.

COLIN. We're out of tins.

ANNE. Get some on the way home then. Christ. Hard tack's bad for them all the time. Hallucinogenic.

COLIN. (*Enters with dustpan, brush.*) What?

ANNE It blows their feline minds. Doctor was saying: three weeks on that hard tack and their cat was found cowering in front of a mouse.

COLIN. (*Brushes up floor round bed.*) Now for the bad news. What I found in the vomit. A goldfinch head.

ANNE. Oh no.

COLIN. Stupid bitch of a cat. It'd be tolerable if she'd at least done it in the honour of digesting it. Most beautiful songbird in Europe, what a waste. They chose our garden for their home. At their nesting they worked so hard. Collaborated so well. For their eggs and— (*Silence.*)

ANNE. Better go and clean it up. (*Takes clean tissue, explores.*)

COLIN. I've not the time now. (*Tie half-tied, snatches jacket.*)

ANNE. It'll stink the place out, flies'll come in, it'll stain— (*Brings out tissue; very red.*)

COLIN. I'm supposed to be playing for Assembly this morning. (*Sees tissue, offers basket.*) Your egg'll be cold.

ANNE. (*Wipes hand on blanket-corner.*) I don't want it.

COLIN. Eat it. You're getting no lunch, you know that. (*Goes out with dustpan, brush.*)

ANNE. (*Taps egg.*) Egg smells funny. (*Beheads egg with knife. Suddenly a most convulsive recoil—she hurls herself from bed, reels down—with a shock we see her nightdress stained where she bleeds. Crouches shuddering, utterly upturned. COLIN re-enters; sees her gone; looks into egg. Utters almost inaudible choke of abomination; covers egg with first thing to hand; stands, bottling nausea, shock.*)

ANNE. (*To self.*) What am I trying to save? Some monster to be born, they'll take one look at— (*COLIN stumbles away Out with egg. LIGHT CHANGE; ANNE feels belly, wondering what horror might be forming there.*) Or a Mozart, Darwin? My will is blind. But is it itself willed, by some other Will, that sees? That wills into being— Man's share of monstrosity or his share of light? Is it either of these? Or is the world's will wild? Without mercy, senseless? At the heart of things, what if there *is* no purpose, no logic, no love at all? (*LIGHT now favours Down Left area. ANNE by bed, back to us, slowly dons a plain long-worn dressing gown [from chair]. COLIN comes bringing a garden lounger, unfolds this, erects it Down Stage; dressed as returned from school.*)

COLIN. (*No sarcasm.*) Have you thought how lucky we are? Think how lucky. Think of the rabbit. She ovulates every time she's entered. Homo sapiens is at least some way advanced on that. Perhaps you and I and others in our predicament are one stage even more evolved.

ANNE. (*Eases self carefully onto lounger, head Left.*) Right now I'd rather be a dodo bird.

COLIN. (*Tucks her in.*) Extinction hurts too. We're wrong to patronize the dinosaur, by the way. One of the kids was saying. The dinosaur lasted five hundred times longer than Man is likely to. It seems Man's last end, though, will be the moral same. (*Cleans away remaining rubbish by bed.*)

ANNE. Out of step with his environment.

COLIN. Worse than that. It seems there were tiny termites, millions of them, eating their way up the Dinosaur's legs. His nerve-system was so slow, out of touch with his condition, the pain didn't reach the brain till all his nethers were eaten away. (*Anne reaches out another bloodied tissue, COLIN automatically brings down basket.*) So what are *our* termites? What danger-signal is the human brain not getting? (*Goes. VALERIE, Young Married from ONE, breezes down In.*)

VALERIE. Coo-ee, folks!

ANNE. (*Mixed feelings.*) Valerie?

VALERIE. (*She is not pregnant now.*) Anne, my love, you look so pale! (*Her cruelty throughout this scene is pure animal: she deceives her better self she is trying to make ANNE feel a welcome new member to the suffering-wife-and-mother club; she would be 90% horrified if someone were to tell her she was doing the cruel opposite.*) I do hope Colin's cooking's not too awful.

ANNE. Oh his hand's well in now. It *has* been weeks. Anyway, he didn't come straight from his mother's arms to mine.

VALERIE. (*Brings chair, sits.*) You must be ravenous, let me get you something. My poor thing, you're looking so pale! You mustn't let him frazzle you. I know men. He'll try to make you feel guilty because he has to knuckle to for once like a domestic martyr; he'll look at you accusingly because you're out of action bleeding your guts out.

ANNE. They're his guts as well in a way I'm bleeding out.

VALERIE. Don't let him. You need calm, peace of mind. I'll make some coffee. (*Goes out.*)

ANNE. Heard about that man arrested in Brum the other day? Blowing bubbles in the street? He got fined. For 'obstruction.' I want this untimely little bastard if he lives to be a blower of bubbles, Christ I do. (*Quiet and more to self.*) Oh, I don't know. You bring a kid up anarchist, he ends up joining the police. How do you bring a spirit up to be free? Shove his tongue up the anus of Authority and trust to his instinct for revolt? Manipulation, that. Hell's teeth, why hang my hang-ups round the necks of the unborn? (*Addressing belly.*) Bloodbeast. Take over the graveyard in your own good time and your own right. If you see our values have failed us, cack on our graves. (VALERIE *returns with coffee cups on tray.*)

VALERIE. Look pleased to see me.

ANNE. (*Meaning no slight.*) I'm pleased to see anybody, stuck like this.

VALERIE. Thank *you!* (*They drink. Pause.* VALERIE: *a new tone—a we-women can't win confidence is coming:*) Speaking of bastards. (*Pause.*) You're not the only one with troubles. *I'm* over*due.* I know I shouldn't be saying this to you in your condition, but what I've been through—! I don't *want* it, Anne; I can't have it; well I can't, can I? How can I? It isn't George's, it's Fred's. Oh I *know* . . . What's so awful, we've only slept together once this cycle—

ANNE. You have it easy, all you have to do is sleep together—!

VALERIE. But isn't it rotten, such rotten luck, Anne? I can't tell you how sorry for you both I am: I wake up thinking how pale you both are, your pale faces, and you were so healthy before you married and so *happy* . . . God, in the old days Colin— (*Tears forgotten.*) on that Lambretta—Looking so brown— (COLIN *comes, utterly unselfconsciously tying on a woman's apron.*)

COLIN. (*Pointed.*) Ah, here's the tray—

VALERIE. Colin! (*Sees apron; incredulous shriek.*) Colin! I never thought to see the day!

COLIN. What? Oh this. (*Camps slightly, to trap her.* VALERIE *utters a camp giggle,* ANNE *wryly watches.*) Yes, you *would* think it funny. I just happen to be weird: I don't see how it is manlier somehow, to let one's clothes get wet. (*Takes tray, leaving cups.*)

VALERIE. (*Shouts after.*) I didn't say anything about your not being virile, Colin! Lord, how should I know? (*Turns to Anne, resumes we-women-can't-win tune.*) God, the trouble I had, carrying Jason. He simply *refused* to be born. George was driving me over railroad crossings, foreways and backways, the little bugger simply refused to be born. Christ, when he did come, such a relief, my dear: to be able to see your toes again. (COLIN *heard clattering rather pointedly in kitchen Off.*) Ah well. When you're up and about again, my dear, you must come and have tea with me and the children, and we'll have a jolly old cow. (*Stands, whispers.*) Don't let him *frazzle* you, dear. (*Calls.*) By-ee! (*Goes.* COLIN *emerges, jabs thumb in her departed direction.*)

COLIN. When my mother was in the Royal Victoria having that breast off, there was an old biddy from Ballymacarrett sat up on high pillows opposite her all the day, dangling . . . (*Gestures.*) . . . her full pair over the bedclothes. For cruelty, of all the sexes, women are the worst. (*Kisses* ANNE, *takes cups, goes.* ANNE *questioningly feels her belly; is troubled.* COLIN *comes, sits on chair, aproned still. Quiet:*) I never know what I'll find instead of you when I get home. And at night: I sleep deeper than hell, yet the slightest shift of you, I'm full sharp awake— (*Pause.*)

ANNE. It wakes me too, the blood.

COLIN. My frazzle didn't make you any better. My frazzle at the beginning is part of the fault of it.

ANNE. (*To disabuse him.*) I lost a little at the *second* month. (*Each suddenly conscious of irremediable personal separateness.*)

COLIN. My anxiety made you worse. That's why I slowed up. Anyway, we can have wrong things invested in a child.

ANNE. I know.

COLIN. If he or she is born, then he or she is born. If it is a matter of your will only, he shall be born. It's easy for me. I've everything to do. You've nothing but to lie, lie, willing. (*Would pat her belly.*)

ANNE. (*Gently stays his hand. Pause.*) I think it's died. (*Long silence. Helpless.*) There isn't the little flutter any more.

COLIN. (*At last.*) Maybe it's just lying quiet a while. They do that, don't they? (*Pause.*) Or playing possum. Perhaps he's realized, it's life or death: so he just daren't rock the boat—too—vigorously . . . (*Pause. Brisk.*) What simple task for you can I find, won't overtax your inferior domestic-female mind? (*Goes. Reappears with bowl of washed spuds, saucepan, spud-basher, newspaper for peelings.*) For thick wife: 'Put ze rett triankles in ze rett boxes, and ze green ones in ze green boxes.' (ANNE *seizes spudbasher in fist, pulls a neolithic gesture.* COLIN *sits on chair* VALERIE *has left. They begin peeling.*) That Professor Eysenck book, by the way, "*Know Your Own IQ*", I found a mistake. Well not a mistake so much: an omission. Very revealing. He has a question: 'Fill in ze missink letters. H, E, blank, I, T, A, blank, E.'

ANNE. (*Thinks. Does her idiot act.*) Artichoke. (*They peel on a few moments.*)

COLIN. No, think. (*Writes with finger on paper.*) H E blank I T A blank E.

ANNE. (*Studies paper as though letters were present there. At last.*) I can do the picture ones, I can't do the word ones. I'm illiterate, I can't spell English, I didn't do any Latin at school.

COLIN. (*Pause. Exaggerated Ulster tone.*) H. E. Blank. I. T. A. Blank. E.

ANNE. (*Immediate.*) Heritage.

COLIN. Heritage. So I thought. But not our father Eysenck. For him the word is hesitate. For Eysenckian man Inheritance does not exist—except as a congenital tic. In behaviorist Utopia we do not belong, we conform; we do not inherit, we obey. Who does not do so, electric treatment shall put right. Heritage my arse. He-si-tate. To stutter to stammer to stumble to *be unsure, that,* in the Eysenck cosmos, is our determined role.

ANNE. Perhaps he just forgot.

COLIN. The man who'd speak from Sinai, has no business 'forgetting.'

ANNE. Did you switch 'oven on? (COLIN *has forgotten, goes.* ANNE *quietly moves paper, peelings a little down, rests hand on belly. Uneasy. From under pillow takes out a clean tissue. Makes cautious assay beneath blanket. Brings tissue out; no visible stain, yet something on it she does not like. She looks carefully, sniffs, folds tissue carefully, stows into dressing gown pocket. Settles to continue peeling, uneasy. After a moment tries to steepen headrest behind her head but, without knowing, jerks it too far forward before resting it carefully back at what she thinks is a new angle. Does not lean back immediately, but brings paper, peelings, potatoes, etc., back into reach, leans back, headrest falls flat, she with it. A cry. After a moment she sees she will have to ease self off lounger to adjust headrest. Clumsily, not daring bend her body, she manoeuvres stiff self sideways off lounger— her foot fouls spudbowl; spuds, water spill; she collapses onto knees amid wet and dirt, heavy, crumpled, breathless.* COLIN *comes quietly, sees.*)

COLIN. (*Annoyed she didn't call for help.*) You hopeless woman. (*Starts to clear mess.*)

ANNE. I'm all wet.

COLIN. You've coggled the bowl, I'm not surprised you're wet.

ANNE. (*Without turning to him, hand to belly.*) No,

here I'm wet. (*Pause.*) My waters have broken. (*Turns her face up to him. A still moment.*) AMBULANCE DRIVER, *gentle, heavy-sized, comes unfolding a stretcher.* COLIN *goes to collect what* ANNE *will need in hospital: no flap with him, all is smooth now.* DRIVER *lays stretcher out on floor between bed and lounger.*)

DRIVER. (*Deeper rural accent, perhaps Birmingham-tarnished, than* DOCTOR *had.*) Now don't you worry, dear. We'll get you there quick as we can. By the smooth road. We know all the bumps in the County, don't you worry. (*Rolls bedclothes onto* COLIN's *half of bed, revealing naked rostrum; then gently helps* ANNE *onto stretcher.*) This lady now sees, for the first time she fully sees: she'm in danger of death. Some'at about our sympathy, in how familiar we are with her condition, in how serious and careful it makes us of her, strikes the scale from her eyes. (*Brings bedclothes from lounger, spreads them over* ANNE.) From her bed, from her room, from her little house now we bring her, gentle, gentle on the stretcher— Easy then, Albert. Easy . . . (*Draws stretcher backwards,* ANNE's *head first, toward rostrum.*) Out to the ambulance . . . Ambulance: common enough thing, you say. But to her, to this woman, this ambulance is the valley of the shadow, that sad little shadow through which one in five of British mothers pass. (*Climbs backward up onto rostrum as though up step into ambulance itself: raises stretcher-head, to display* ANNE *to us like a straw guy, undignified, helpless.*) Don't she look like a witch, eh, on her ladder? Or a Jewess, trussed on her tray for the boiler? Her turn now: where others have gone, now she. What other people have, now hers to suffer. Alone. (*Leans stretcherhead on rostrumfoot, crouches on ground, face close to hers. To us.*) Look, a tear. Swells up out of nothing in the socket of her eye. The salt drop from the gland: fills, bulges, quivers. Makes her look so stupid. You could want to smash her face in, for looking so stupid. Weak face, stupid, helpless; slack jaw, so helpless, stupid. It tears your heart in two for pity, and your right hand itches up to strike that stupid face. (*Utterly straight, without pretence.*) There, dear, lie still. We'll get your things together, don't you worry. (COLIN *comes with toiletbag, dressing-gown, slippers, a travel-grip containing nightie, soap, etc.; checks these with* ANNE. DRIVER *to us:*) Beginning to shed; so shove her in gentle. (*Does so.*) Close the doors. (*Draws screen across, masking them all. In apron still,* COLIN *comes slowly; with deliberation clears potatoes, etc., then lounger away behind screen—they will not be needed now. On, Off, unhurrying. At last, in apron still, sits on remaining chair. To self:*)

COLIN. (*Quiet.*) Now think. Think, how this happens from some good cause. If a bomb or a soldier had done it, you could be bitter. Think, how it can have some—rightness. The way of nature. Yet, was it in the way of nature, what *we* did? Lend her a helping hand. Nature might—take unkindly to our—'help.' I rescued a shrew once, from the cat: yet the shrew ran straight off the shovel into a drain. The struggling in the water; the sound of the little blind thing struggling in the water. 'Helped.' It is true: what happens to us in the world, bears no resemblance to 'morality.' Yet, from that—inequity, might there not be a lesson to be learned? We are so near the letters, how can we see the word? (*Silence.*) In nature there is no annihilation. The dead are eaten. What remains rots down in corruption. In corruption itself murmur the bubbles of rebirth. Even what was burned, from ashes the fields are fertilized. For all that: however a cosmos might absorb calamity, extinction's final for the thing extinct. (*LIGHT CHANGE:* NURSE—*busy little movements—Enters Right, drawing screens into new, hospital-like arrangement.* COLIN *goes slowly up, Off* [*striking lounger, etc., there.*] ANNE *discovered lying on rostrum—now hospital bed, its foot towards us.* NURSE *raises* ANNE's *head on pillows, continues Off.* ANNE *lies listless, telling us:*)

ANNE We thought we'd saved it. The cervix contracted, it almost closed. One of the doctors, had hobnailed boots on his fingers: whenever he examined me— (*Breath fails in remembered pain.*) I'd only to *see* it was him on the wards, I'd start to bleed— But we thought we'd saved it. They even told Colin, 'Come in with her clothes tomorrow, she'll be all right.' But when he came, with the suitcase, 'We're sorry,' they said: 'she's had a bad night; she must stay a while longer.' One morning they rang him. 'Your wife's going down to the theatre,' they said. He saw what that meant. 'I see,' he said: 'for the scrape, you mean.' 'Scrape?' they said. 'Well, if we've lost the baby—' he said. 'Baby?' they said: 'what baby?' They looked in the records: 'It *is* Mr. Harvey?' 'Harding,' he said. 'Oh. Harding. Oh no, Mr. Harding, oh I *am* sorry, oh no, Mrs. Harding's perfectly all right—' He was always last out of Visiting. One night, five minutes after he left, I wanted a crap. I called for the bedpan. But it wasn't a crap. It was just as easy as a crap. Easier. Plop, it was out— (*Scream.*) Nurse! (*DARKNESS. ON SPEAKERS: sounds of comings and goings, a ward emergency, bowls, etc. Bring UP LIGHT, to a blinding white: screen behind* ANNE's *head, a blinding white.* ANNE's *face a terrible white, eyes red.* COLIN *quietly brings chair up to bedside, pathetic bunch of wild [as named—NB must look authentic] flowers in his hand.* NURSE *goes.*)

COLIN. The ditches are white with stitchwort. (*Shows.*) Herb Robert. Cranesbill. Campion. (*Gives.*)

ANNE. (*No list to take them.*) There were two. Two babies. One came, then I was unconscious; then the other, it woke me in the night. I said 'Is it a boy?' 'Nothing,' she said, 'it's only clots.' But it was a baby. I know it was. There were two. They were twins. One must have gone wrong, you see. One must have been wrong from the start. So it died in the womb, it brought them both out, the good one with the bad. (*Motionless throughout.*) The nurse won't tell me. I only want to know it wasn't a monster. Or that it *was* a monster. I don't know what it is I want to know. (*Pause.*) They're in the fridge. They take them to the end of the ward and—put them in the fridge. In the next ward you can hear the good ones crying, the ones that have been born. You have to have the different gyny wards together, that's only sense . . .

COLIN. Next ward's where we'll be. Next time.

ANNE. (*Motionless, seems not to hear him.*) I said to the doctor, I won't go through all this again. Oh he's a patronising bastard, the nurses queue up to kiss his arsehole—he's only a *doctor!* I won't go through this again, I told him: bugger this for a tale. Next time I start to bleed I'll go down to my husband's school and hire the trampoline.

COLIN. Next time we'll be in there. This happens to one couple in five first time. We'll be in there next time.

ANNE. (*Utterly motionless. At last.*) He said—
'There isn't going to be a next time, Mrs. Harding.
I'm sorry. We have had to take the womb away.'
(*Pause.*) 'I'm sure your GP will recommend you for
adoption.' (*Silence.* ANNE *suddenly buries head in*
COLIN'S *breast:*) I'm sorry, love, I'm sorry—

COLIN. (*Stunned.*) Why 'sorry'—?

ANNE. (*Something indistinct, i.e., about giving
children.*)

COLIN. (*Can find nothing to say but.*) No . . .
No . . . (*i.e., stop saying sorry.*) .

ANNE. (*Something indistinct, i.e., about wanting to
have* his *children—*)

COLIN. No, no . . . Stop being so Arab. It's not
'giving children,' it's having. *Our* children, not mine.
No. No.

ANNE. (*Constrained movement, orchestrating her
pinned anguish.*) I can see the smoke. From the incin-
erator. Burning my womb—! (*They remain, motionless, silent. At last:*)

COLIN. (*Very quiet.*) Gone then. Gone. Gone. We
must do what we can with what remains. All that, is
gone. (ANNE *utters one high-inaudible gasp of grief.
Shakes bitterly, silent. Deathly quiet.*) Gone. (*They
remain so, motionless, silent, a cruel time. Then CUT
LIGHT.*)

Chill pp MUSIC, spare, groping, desolate (Epilogue Vaughan Williams VI): in darkness strike screen, bedclothes; move bare rostrum Up Right unpresent. Soon lifeless LIGHTPOOL DOWN MID: FADE VW. On chair sits Social Services OFFICER—mid 30's, compassionate, quite smooth; suit clerical grey, duplicated notes on crossed thighs. Behind him a large colourless map of unidentifiable county divided into two or three contrastingly-shaded admin regions. OFFICER's chin on a steeple of his hands: he eyes his audience, now this couple, now that (in real life seated in nervous semicircle before him) perceivingly. Near him, slightly Upstage of and out of alignment with him, seated on other chair AREA ADOPTIONS OFFICER, a woman in early 30's, smart, conventional, attractive; clipboard on lap. She would be discreetly watching this couple, now that; noting a reaction here, a give-away gesture there; one or twice she will, all but imperceptibly, make a brief mark on her list of names, while OFFICER speaks:

OFFICER. (*Gentle, absolute, enshrining a hardness: he must prepare his hearers for the worst.*) We, in the Authority, realize you come to us as a last resort. We accept that. You have discovered for yourselves, there is no 'host of unwanted children' awaiting adoption: This application you have lodged with us is thus virtually your last chance for parenthood of any kind. If then, as I speak, you are furtively assessing these other couples' chances with us as against your own,

that is only understandable. For you know this is not
a rivalry so much between you; yet you know also—
if not, you are not ready for adoption—to adopt
means, not to find a child you think suits you, but for
us the County to find a home we think right for the
child. Thus in the nature of things we can never say
yes to you all. Even those of you, brave enough to
offer a home to a child of other or mixed race, or to a
child in some way handicapped, we shall almost always have to turn away. There are not the children.
Sad then though your path has so far been, it may yet
lead to further sadness. We share that sadness. You
come to adoption because you have had to accept that
natural parenthood is a common human heritage from
which you are shut out. You have had to rethink parenthood; perforce matured, into seeing a possible child
of yours, not as a product of yourself, but as an infant
person already possessed of his or her own history,
bringing it with him, absolute in his own right. You
have learned, a hard way, that in true parenthood
there is no fantasy, no self-extension, no fond notion
of vertical inheritance of what you think is best in
you: you leave such fatuous hopes behind, evolving
perhaps, towards a parenthood of tomorrow. But. If
you have had cause for painful self-search before, I
must warn you there is more to come. You would not
feel safe in committing yourself to a child of whom you
knew nothing: still less can we hazard a child to a
home of whose history values and likely future we had
not found out all we reasonably could. You must be
prepared, for prolonged and deep investigation: medical, professional, financial; marital. You will flinch
from this inquisition; at times feel laid out on our slab
just once too often. Appreciate our reasons. Nor is it

pleasant for us, submitting a man's or a woman's deepest motives to dissection. Our Area Officer, Mrs. Jones, who shares this casework, will endorse me on this. AREA OFFICER *makes discreet minimal acknowledgment.*) Be warned. Expect little. Even if in the end we find you would make a most excellent couple for our list, it might still be most unlikely such a child will become available to us, as you will suit. In such a case, we prefer to get your disappointment over and done with straight away. Our reasons, however, for not accepting you, we never give. Painful though it is, to be found unsuitable and left wondering for ever why, we find that on balance it is safer for you, to be left in the dark. We marvel constantly at the courage would-be adoptive parents show. You begin to see now, how much you really need. (*LIGHT SHRINKS:* OFFICER, AREA OFFICER *quietly go UP; map stays. From DARKNESS, pale, naked but for pale-blue briefs, comes slowly* COLIN *down to chair: in his hand, black leather shoes [in them, rolled-up socks], over his arm a vest, white linen shirt, black tie, light cardigan of fawn wool, black funeral suit.*)

COLIN. (*As he slowly dresses.*) Last time I wore this, was over in Ireland, too. Some country. Some 'Mother.' Only cause can bring us flying back to her is death . . . Poor Uncle Tommy. 'Fine fella of a mahn.' To end in pieces. What sort of son am I, to such fine fathers? White sterile son, dead branch of the tribe . . . No. No. All that's behind me. Progenitive fantasy, all behind me. For fatherhood I was not made. Nature was wise, she cast me from the start: dead seed, best fit to mix with excrement—ashes to ashes. (*Sarcastic.*) But I knew better. 'I knowed better.' I would be a 'mahn.' A 'father.' With cold water and bicarbonate of soda, chart calendar and clock— 'Hi, oul' bitch Nature!' I said, 'I'll worst ye yet!' If I had been content— (*Pauses.*) Content . . . (*Sees truth of it.*) Content . . . my wife would have her womb this day. 'Application for Adoption. Name, birthdate, address, profession, religion—none; average income, size of house, medical history—likelihood suddenly to die; biographical remarks— (*Self-mocking.*) I wrote them half a novel there . . . Two independent referees outside the family . . . First interview, the two of us, here. Next interview, there, myself alone: 'Mr. Harding, how genuinely motivated for parenthood do you think you are?' (*He is dressed now. Sits on chair, black suit emphasizing his pallor, his longing:*) A child to come to us, absolute in his own right, his own inheritance, free of ours . . . Real child, a daughter, a son, real . . . Real flesh, real self, real person, real . . . to come to us, sidelong . . . Not down from us, but out, across the world, to us . . . (*After a moment he goes up into DARKNESS.* AREA OFFICER *Mrs. Jones comes with file to sit where she sat before;* ANNE, *pale, nervous, in drab camel coat, comes to sit in other chair, almost facing her. She takes off coat, her frock a bloodred shock, as though the blood on the tissue had grown through the stain on her nightdress to become all of her.* AREA OFFICER'S *tone throughout is utterly unrevealing, objective; quiet, compassionate, but searching. She hardly takes her eyes off* ANNE *at all.*)

AREA OFFICER. Mrs. Harding. How strongly do you want to become a parent?

ANNE. I think our history answers that.

AREA OFFICER. You have shown remarkable perseverance. When I spoke to your husband, he said how much he admired your willpower when you lay there— how did he put it? —'willing your foetus to stay in place.' I thought he too had from the beginning shown quite frightening willpower. Why do you think he did so?

ANNE. For fatherhood.

AREA OFFICER. Simply that?

ANNE. (*Thinking.*) For Colin, fatherhood isn't a simple thing— Whenever I go to an interview I end up talking about him. It was the same when I was trying for the stage: at auditions we ended up talking about him. He used to write plays.

AREA OFFICER. (*Faintest wintry humour.*) We talked about you last week.

ANNE. Yes. When he got home I asked him how it went. 'Lousy,' he said, 'I reckon I talked our child away.'

AREA OFFICER. (*Silent. Then:*) How do you think he would react, if we were to turn down your application, knowing that with it there almost certainly goes your last chance?

ANNE. (*Thinks. Then:*) He'd be very bitter. Then he'd accept. What else? We'd both accept. Then move on.

AREA OFFICER. Away?

ANNE. Oh no. I mean, if we're not to be parents, move on to what we *can* become.

AREA OFFICER. (*Pause.*) What do you think is your husband's worst fault?

ANNE. Pigheadedness. It's a sort of—Protestant integrity, but it comes over as pigheadedness.

AREA OFFICER. When he discovered he had no future as a writer, he didn't resist that. He turned away and started another life.

ANNE. Thousands do that. I did that.

AREA OFFICER. If we were to refuse you, what would your reaction be?

ANNE. (*Has pondered this already.*) It would all seem part of the—evolving pattern. (*Sees* AREA OFFICER *would like her to amplify.*) When our careers collapsed, his and mine, we began to read it as a sort of message, if you like: that we ought to—take a different road. We came out here; we went back to teaching, for which we'd both been trained; we became rural and domestic. Soon the idea of children became important. Well you know what happened about *that.* So. If we were turned down, it would be pretty conclusive this was a wrong road, too. (*Long silence.*)

AREA OFFICER. How strong do you think your marriage is? (ANNE *thinks.*) What do you think is the greatest threat to it?

ANNE. (*At last.*) If one knew that . . .

AREA OFFICER. Your husband's answer to this question was: (*Brief glance at notes.*) 'When the earthquake happens, the buildings that survive are the ones that swayed.' How do you think he means, your marriage could sway? His rather unorthodox sexuality, you think because of that?

ANNE. I don't think he meant the *marriage* could sway. I think he meant about people rolling with the punches that Nature gives them.

AREA OFFICER. Yet you say he is pigheaded.

ANNE. (*Candid.*) He's learning. (*Yes: she has been the stronger all along.*) Anyway. I don't think his sexuality is unorthodox. His acknowledgment of it might be. We have to tell you these things.

AREA OFFICER. That he can consciously feel for his own sex, do you think that threatens your marriage?

ANNE. I feel safer.

AREA OFFICER. Safer?

ANNE. Safer than if he had a roving eye for other

women. Anyway, I've told him: if he has to have a bit of the other sex once in a while, just be sure to come back clean. It's how he's made; he has only one life. Likewise me. If I *have* to succumb to the milkman, he says Just not in *our* bed. It's a joke but . . . a grain of truth. If that shocks you, I'm sorry.

AREA OFFICER. It doesn't shock me—

ANNE. We don't abuse each other's liberality— Anyway, men with open homosexual emotions are supposed to make good fathers. It's just a rotten consequence of natural logic so few of them get the chance.

AREA OFFICER. Is your marriage satisfactory, Mrs. Harding?

ANNE. Bed, you mean.

AREA OFFICER. Among other things.

ANNE. Not always. In fact, it's rather bad just now. The tension all this has put us under. And the fact that I shall never conceive does—to begin with, anyway—make some difference. He's not the great greasy bullock of my dreams, what woman's husband is? It's probably better to find your man tolerable company for fifty years than be hooked on his cock. I don't even like my husband all the time: but for good or ill he's in my belly now.

AREA OFFICER. (*At last.*) What do you think you have to offer a child, Mrs. Harding?

ANNE. (*Thinks a long time. Then:*) Nothing; specific. Just what we'd have to offer children of our own. I can't think of anything. Just a—share in living. (*CUT LIGHT. ON speakers: sudden AIRPORT SOUND, loud aircraft landing. In DARKNESS strike map, bring bare rostrum Mid-Centre, set chairs as front seats in a van. DING-DONG, VOICE of airport announceress: 'BEA announce the arrival of flight number BE 425 from Belfast.' Repeat. SOUNDS of airport corridor, many people trooping. FADE AIR-CRAFT SOUNDS. Two CAR DOORS SLAM: SOUND of IGNITION, car pulling away. UP FAINT-EST LIGHT.* Colin, Anne *sit as in van, he passenger in coat, she with minimal mime—perhaps false steering wheel necessary—driving.*)

Colin. (*Trying for thousandth time to realify the horror to himself.*) They all stood, paralyzed. Someone had said 'There's a second bomb, keep away.' But after a minute they could bear the tension no longer; they all rushed forward. In. They say the scene that met their eyes was—unspeakable. Pieces of people, hunks of unrecognizable torn flesh; pathetic items of shopping, clothes, school books; a boy's head. The nethers of a pregnant woman, skewered on a bus-stop shaft. Atrocious anagram of people going home. Somewhere in that, Uncle Tommy had died. To that conclusion, his days had been bringing him all along. Aunt Annie said, 'So why did ye stay across the water so long?' 'Ye knew ye could have come live wi us why did ye not come here?' she said: 'wi us?' I said: Because I was afeared. Truth to tell, Aunt Annie, I was afeared to come. Besides, because I am so torn. 'Between what?' Torn, I tried to tell her, torn wondering where best—no, not where best; where at all we go now. 'Aunt Annie'—my heart was in my mouth as I said it— 'we've known from year one our old North of Ireland had to go some time.' I have always known trouble would come in that country. When the riots broke out, I was disturbed: I began to wonder. Awful to say, only the bombs have made me really think. If an undertribe can commit themselves to such atrocity, there must be some terrible misery they are trying to communicate. And our . . . (*Searches self deeply for these words:*) inequity . . . monopoly of things . . . self— (*This last word he almost fails to find. Self-satisfaction, no. Tries again.*) Self— (*Still cannot find. At long last, after appalling self-search.*) certainty . . . (*Pause.*) Self-certainty and acquiescence . . . add up to a muckheap only violence will shift. Sure, we've known all along our old ways had to go. Some time. The reckoning come. Some time. The whirlwind. In someone's time. The whirlwind is here. In our time. We went into the room at the back of the house where—what is left of Lily Martin lives. Aunt Annie had tried to prepare me: 'You not show your shock, now.' I clapped eyes on—that trunk of her, no legs, no arms; the head as bald as an egg, half the features blown away. The breath was dashed out of me, I had no breath left to try to—hide my horror. And Lily saw. Three hours out of the twenty-four she'll sleep now; the other twenty-one she cries. Cousin Sammy came, was, and is, to marry her. He stood beneath the picture of the Duke of Edinburgh and the Queen: 'It's well for you,' he said, 'across the water. We here have to fight. To save the land we love.' I wanted to say There are other ways to fight. I wanted to say This way of yours, what shall you do to this 'land you love?' I wanted to say Do I not love this land as well as you? —I love that land; her I carry . . . But . . . Violence will never pay, we are told. But it does; and in our hearts we know it does. I: have been part of a muck that only violence can shift. Yet I said to Sam 'Soon or late, this violence must end': I said 'I just think we have to change somehow, to try to find some new way, up, out of this. Sammy,' I tried to say, 'we have been a great people. Twice in history our

Protestant existence here has turned a tide of tyranny back: now we are on the anvil a third time. Can we rise to the occasion this third time, then? turn a third tyranny back? the tyranny of our own— (*Now it hits* COLIN, *and the clarity of it is freeing him:*) *inheritance?* Our inheritance is glorious, we are a— But all that has to be behind us now. Shed. I just—I just think we just have to—try to see, what new selves we can rise up out of this, and become. Oh, Sammy, if we can do that, oh then we are a brave tribe.' (*Perhaps with a hint of Sammy's up-you gesture:*) 'Phoenix yerself.' Uncle Tommy's coffin lay in the front parlour of the house, for friends and neighbours to come filing in to see: 'Lord bless us but he makes a lovely corpse.' Only Tommy's coffin was closed. Tommy's was closed. One of the neighbour-women even said: 'Your Tommy was a large mahn. His coffin is so small.' In the morning, the men all came to carry him to his grave. I went to put my shoulder to the coffin to do my share of the bearing. The men pushed me aside. And Sam said— (*Quiet, reasonable:*) 'You'll carry no Ulsterman's coffin to no grave. Stay here wi the weemen.' The drum beat. Up the street, to the Orange Hall then to the grave, went with that coffin all my—belonging . . . The women did not speak to me. I felt so severed. (*No self-pity, but an absolute new clear-seeing:*) I know it is the strongest feeling in the world, to be alone. And I did feel strong. Yet, the land, from whose earth I belong, the clan, from whose loins I come, had turned me out; to my own loins no child of tomorrow shall come: and I felt so— (*At last.*) severed. (*Long silence: he takes out, lights, a cigarette [only time anyone smokes in entire play]. Peers out of side-window into dark. For him, though a sorrow, it is also a setting free:*) So.

There's another—'self' for the rubbish heap with all
the rest. My self as 'tribal son.' Yet: if we do not
change, tomorrow has no place for us. (*CUT LIGHT.
On speakers: wide-spaced PIANO-ARPEGGI, in slow
five-finger groups, stepwise haltingly ascend, descend
in C major, C minor, A flat major; D flat, etc. STRIKE
chairs. SLOW FADE UP COLD LIGHT: a wheel-
barrow with newdug potatoes, ANNE in camel-coat
seated on rostrum-foot carefully sorting—those cut or
speared in digging, into a box or basket, for immediate
use; the good, gently into a bulging ½cwt paper sack;
the blighted, onto a spread local newspaper, for dis-
carding.*)

ANNE. Bloody piano. 'Exercise to stretch the webs
between the fingers.' Why won't he *accept* his hands
are too small? In winter his skin hardens, the webs
split and bleed. I begin to wonder: does he only try at
what he knows he can't achieve? Some sort of escape,
that. Lord grant me learn my proper parish . . .
(*FADE PIANO OUT meanwhile. A blighted potato
breaks between ANNE's finger and thumb:*) Irishman,
and these he grows. (*Puts it onto paper.*) Still . . .
Blight. Good years and bad. Luck . . . Husbandry . . .
I could gorge between my legs now the milk of a
thousand men and it all perish, safe. Stop; stop.
Burn these. (*An advert in paper catches her eye:*)
'What is it makes the Arnolds so full of pep?' (*Wry,
resuming work.*) What *is* it, makes the Arnolds so full
of pep? (*Becomes conscious of a sound we do not
hear:*) Elms being felled. All the parks fields farms of
the county, elms being felled. Bark stripped off and
burnt, roots ripped up and burnt. Along the roads their
tall crowns wither, grow bald, their doomed stems
marked with a white painted cross. And the farmers

burn the stubble all over, day and night—when by
law they should not—to burn the wheat-rust out. And
because it's cheaper. Singe the orchards, burn the
hedgerows with their buds and berries down, because
it's cheaper. Pillage the earth, and before it's rested,
radge it with a winter crop. Squeeze the earth dry,
she'll last just about as long as we shall; bugger our
sons. (*Elsewhere, another sound we do not hear:*) Jeff
Walton, altering his pigs he's bought. They grub their
own testicles up from the ground where they've fallen,
and eat them. I just remember my dream. I was teaching the children. Suddenly I said 'Oh children, all you
children, go under, all go under, quickly, quickly.' Outside it was bright blue day. Such blue. Suddenly I saw
in the sky huge vessels, shaped like the upturned
abdomens of wasps, striped yellow-and-red, yellow-
and-green, upcurling and vanishing into the blue. I
knew what they were. The air was clammy with a fine
invisible mist, in the sunshine all the people shopping
had begun to vomit and spit. I ran to the chemist's for
a sink to puke in but his door was padlocked. In all
the house-windows, notices: Clean Water 5p. I came
home. I said, 'Colin, I did what I could, I brought
home what I could.' But in my basket there was
nothing. I cried at that. I cried such tears, the wild
upwelling that we weep in dreams. He was trying to
make love to me. His penis was arid and red hot. I was
pretending. Suddenly he screamed and leapt away
from me, bent over. 'Oh what's the matter my love?' I
said; 'tell me the matter.' He said—when the seed
came out of him, it was scalding spit, it tore out of his
knob like the E string of a violin—and I saw: it had
ripped up and back along his shaft like a cheesewire.
I touched him: I wanted to make him better, I touched

him, his flesh turned hard, then scaly like a fish. I
could see he was dying. He was dying— Then he was
dead. I came out across the marsh. The sky was red
like blood. The land was black. The cabbages had
been blasted from their stalks, the stalks stood gnarled
and knotted in rows, unnaturally gleaming. I was
weak. I could see my body was turning scaly as his
had done. I dragged myself to where I could lean
against a thorntree. I lay there. A child came. No child
that I would call a child. A child of ice, moving without seeming to move, crossing the black flat of the
marsh beneath the red sky. He-she-it, featureless,
white, its head in a dome like a child from space. I
was so frightened, so weak I could not lift myself at
all; I felt I was going out, like water down a drain:
into extinction. (*Thinks, does not say: "But no." New
tone of coming resurrection:*) I woke. A voice over-
lapped from the dream: the child's and mine: the
same. 'Take *off* your dead.' (*Quietly* COLIN *comes, in
anorak, cords again; opened letter in hand.*)

COLIN. (*Terse.*) From the County. (*Face, voice show
nothing.* ANNE *snatches letter, glancing at his face;
then reads.* COLIN *leans arms upon rostrum-side, reading paper without taking any of it in; a covert glance
at* ANNE. *She is looking up, forward, out, letter in hand
on lap.* COLIN *waits till it is time for him to speak:
[not cold; but inly stricken of all expression].*) That's
it. Another 'us' to shed: mummy and daddy. (*Looks
down at paper again. Eye catches something. With
tiniest chuckle:*) 'Day-old boy found in lavatory pan
in Worcester.' The world is like this. (ANNE *says
nothing.* COLIN *does not look up. A there-it-is tone.*)
Laughter of children in our house, not for us. Whatever
is. (*Yes. Whatever is. This road must now be aban-*

doned also. ANNE *sees it; inly she has known it all along. It is pitiful, but they are released. Their hopes for parenthood lie in ashes, but on some other road must lie whatever is for them. After a moment she turns herself, without standing, toward* COLIN; *with right hand she quite strongly seizes his hair, forcefully raises his face to her own. On his face suddenly the beginning of a strange light. CUT immediately.)*

THE END